books by
BOXER

www.booksbyboxer.com

Published by
Books By Boxer, Leeds, LS13 4BS UK
Books by Boxer (EU), Dublin D02 P593 IRELAND
© Books By Boxer 2022
All Rights Reserved
MADE IN CHINA
ISBN: 9781909732582

IF YOU'RE READING THIS, SOMEBODY THINKS YOU NEED TO CHANGE YOUR WAYS BEFORE YOU END UP IN THE SLAMMER.

DON'T WORRY THOUGH, THERE'S STILL TIME TO STOP COMMITTING SOME OF THE WORLD'S WACKIEST CRIMES.

USE THE TALLY TO KEEP TRACK OF HOW LIKELY YOU ARE TO BECOME A NOTORIOUS CRIMINAL.

SUSPICIOUS SALMON

Country of origin: UK

IN THE UK, UNDER SECTION 32 OF THE SALMON ACT 1986, IT IS ILLEGAL TO HANDLE SALMON UNDER 'SUSPICIOUS CIRCUMSTANCES'. WHILST THIS WAS IMPLEMENTED TO COMBAT ILLEGAL FISHING, IT'S STILL FUNNY TO THINK THAT HOLDING A SALMON COULD POTENTIALLY LAND YOU UP TO TWO YEARS IN PRISON – IF YOU GET CAUGHT, THAT IS!

A VERY SUS-FISH-IOUS CRIME INDEED – THOUGH NOT A LIKELY CRIME TO COMMIT! WE'D THINK THIS FISHY LAW WOULD BE PRETTY OBSOLETE BY NOW!

HOW LIKELY ARE YOU TO BREAK THIS LAW?
SCORE YOURSELF OUT OF 10:

RUSSIAN OFF YOUR FEET!

Country of origin: Russia

DATING BACK TO 1907, THERE WAS A SMALL
CHINESE OCCUPIED REPUBLIC NEAR THE
RUSSIAN CITY, VLADIVOSTOK. CALLED
IMAN, THIS SMALL PLACE WAS HOME
TO SOME WILD LAWS! ONE OF THE
ARGUABLY FUNNIEST WAS THAT, BY
LAW, EVERYONE HAD TO ANNOUNCE THE
APPROACH OF A RUSSIAN.

FAILURE TO DO SO? **DEATH** — OF COURSE.
ANOTHER WILD ONE WAS THAT ANYONE
CAUGHT STEALING FUR WAS TO BE BURIED
ALIVE. FAIR ENOUGH IF YOU ASK ME!

HOW LIKELY ARE YOU TO BREAK THIS LAW?
SCORE YOURSELF OUT OF 10:

|||| ||||

FORGET-ME-NOTS!

Country of origin: Samoa

IN SAMOA, THERE IS A LAW THAT STATES
IT'S PUNISHABLE TO FORGET YOUR WIFE'S
BIRTHDAY! ALTHOUGH THIS IS AN OLDER
LAW THAT ISN'T ENFORCED ANYMORE, IT IS
ALMOST CERTAIN THAT IF YOU FORGET YOUR
BELOVED WIFE'S BIRTHDAY, IT'S NOT THE
LAW YOU SHOULD BE SCARED OF!

(MAYBE LIFE IN THE SLAMMER WOULD
BE FOR THE BEST...)

HOW LIKELY ARE YOU TO BREAK THIS LAW?
SCORE YOURSELF OUT OF 10:

~~IIII~~ ~~IIII~~

A WEE BIT SUSPISH

Country of origin: Scotland

IF YOU DENY A STRANGER ACCESS TO YOUR LOO, YOU COULD BE IN SOME DEEP S**T! YES, IN SCOTTISH LAW, YOU ARE LEGALLY OBLIGED TO ALLOW STRANGERS (NO MATTER HOW SHADY) INTO YOUR HOME TO USE THE TOILET IF THEY COME AROUND KNOCKING – SO NEXT TIME YOU'RE BURSTING FOR A PEE, YOU CAN THREATEN THE MEAN OLD LADY WITH POLICE ACTION IF SHE DOESN'T LET YOU IN!

THIS WEE LAW SEEMS A BIT SUS-PISS-IOUS IN ITSELF. LETTING STRANGERS INTO YOUR HOME SO THEY CAN BLOCK YOUR TOILET THEN BE ON THEIR MERRY WAY WITH £5, A TEAPOT AND THREE BOG ROLLS IN HAND? NAY!

HOW LIKELY ARE YOU TO BREAK THIS LAW?
SCORE YOURSELF OUT OF 10:

~~~~ ~~~~

DYING TO GET HERE

Country of origin: Sarpourenx, France

THE SMALL COMMUNE OF SARPOURENX, FRANCE HAD A BIT OF A PROBLEM. YOU SEE, PEOPLE KEPT DYING WITHIN THE TOWN'S WALLS, AND EVEN HAD THE AUDACITY TO WANT TO BE BURIED. THE MAYOR OF THE TOWN, GERARD LALANNE, WASN'T HAVING ANY OF THIS, SO IN 2008 HE CREATED A LAW FORBIDDING PEOPLE FROM DROPPING DEAD WITHIN THE TOWN'S WALLS UNLESS THEY HAD BOUGHT A BURIAL PLOT IN ADVANCE, THREATENING 'SEVERE PUNISHMENT' TO ALL WHO DARED DIE WITHOUT. WHAT A GRAVE PLOT TO DETER TOURISTS WHO ARE JUST DYING TO VISIT!

PLOT TWIST! MAYOR GERARD LALANNE DIED ONLY 10 MONTHS AFTER ISSUING THIS BIZARRE LAW – HOPE HE PAID UP FIRST!

HOW LIKELY ARE YOU TO BREAK THIS LAW?
SCORE YOURSELF OUT OF 10:

HIGH AS A KITE

Country of origin: United Kingdom

DESPITE BEING A FIRM FAVOURITE
ACTIVITY AMONGST FAMILIES, FLYING
A KITE IN PUBLIC PLACES IS HIGHLY
RESTRICTED, WITH MANY UNHEARD OF RULES
AND REGULATIONS THAT WOULD RENDER THIS
MUNDANE ACTIVITY ILLEGAL!

UNDER THE METROPOLITAN POLICE ACT
1839, IT IS ILLEGAL TO FLY A KITE IN
A PUBLIC PLACE "TO THE ANNOYANCE OF
INHABITANTS OR PASSENGERS", AND YOU
MAY BE LIABLE TO A FINE OF UP
TO £500! — TALK ABOUT FLYING LOW
WITHOUT A LICENSE...

WERE THEY HIGH WHEN THEY IMPLEMENTED
THIS LAW? WHY DO THEY INSIST ON
PUTTING A DOWNER ON KITE-FLYING FUN?

HOW LIKELY ARE YOU TO BREAK THIS LAW?
SCORE YOURSELF OUT OF 10:

~~||||~~ ~~||||~~

KFC
(KNIFE, FORK, CHICKEN)

Country of origin: Gainesville, Georgia, USA

IN GAINESVILLE, GEORGIA, IT'S RIGHTEOUSLY ILLEGAL TO EAT FRIED CHICKEN WITH A KNIFE AND FORK! IT'S REPORTED THAT THIS LAW CAME ABOUT IN 1961, LARGELY AS A JOKE TO BRING ABOUT PUBLICITY FOR GAINESVILLE AS BEING THE SELF-PROCLAIMED FRIED CHICKEN CAPITAL OF THE WORLD.

WHILST YOU AREN'T GOING TO GET A CRIMINAL RECORD BY USING YOUR SILVERWARE ON YOUR CHICKEN STRIPS, THE LAW HAS NEVER BEEN OVERTURNED!

HOW LIKELY ARE YOU TO BREAK THIS LAW?
SCORE YOURSELF OUT OF 10:

~~~~| ~~~~|

WOOD YOU IN FOR?

Country of origin: London, England

SORRY TO BREAK IT TO YOU, BUT IF YOU'RE PLANNING ON TAKING YOUR PLANK OF WOOD 'WALKIES' ANYTIME SOON, I'D SUGGEST YOU THINK AGAIN. IN SECTION 54 OF THE METROPOLITAN POLICE ACT, IT STATES THAT CARRYING A PLANK OF WOOD ALONG LONDON PAVEMENTS ISN'T ALLOWED, UNLESS IT'S BEING UNLOADED FROM A VEHICLE, AND YOU CAN ACTUALLY BE FINED A WHOPPING £500.

IF YOU'RE THINKING "I'LL JUST WALK MY LADDERS; WHEELS OR POLES INSTEAD"; THEN I'M AFRAID YOU'LL STILL GET HIT WITH THE SAME CHARGES...

HOW LIKELY ARE YOU TO BREAK THIS LAW?
SCORE YOURSELF OUT OF 10:

PUPPET ON A STRING

Country of origin: New York City, USA

THE FAMOUS PUNCH AND JUDY PERFORMANCE MIGHT BE AN INNOCENT CHILDREN'S PUPPET SHOW, BUT IN NEW YORK, THESE SEEMINGLY INNOCENT PUPPETS COULD HAVE THEIR PUPPET MASTER PUT IN JAIL FOR 30 DAYS! IN FACT, ANYBODY FOUND PUTTING ON "ANY PERFORMANCE OF PUPPET" IN THIS MAJOR CITY WILL BE DETAINED AND PROSECUTED – THAT'S THE WAY TO DO IT!

THEY'VE CERTAINLY TIGHTENED THE STRINGS ON ENTERTAINING THE US POPULATION WITH THIS LAW!

HOW LIKELY ARE YOU TO BREAK THIS LAW?
SCORE YOURSELF OUT OF 10:

||||| ||||

STICKY SITUATION

Country of origin: Indiana, USA

IF YOU LIVE IN INDIANA, AND JUST SO HAPPEN TO BE A GLUE SNIFFER, YOU MIGHT WANT TO LISTEN UP. SNIFFING ANY TOXIC VAPOURS (INCLUDING GLUE) WITH AN "INTENT TO CAUSE A CONDITION OF INTOXICATION, EUPHORIA, EXCITEMENT, EXHILARATION, STUPEFACTION, OR DULLING OF THE SENSES" IS AGAINST THE LAW, AND YOU COULD BE PROSECUTED AND CHARGED FOR YOUR CRIME. IF YOU'RE SNIFFING IT FOR A DIFFERENT REASON THOUGH, WELL… WHO ARE WE TO JUDGE?

THE GLUE SNIFFERS OF INDIANA WILL BE STUCK IN A RUT, WITH NO-STRIL WAY OUT!

HOW LIKELY ARE YOU TO BREAK THIS LAW?
SCORE YOURSELF OUT OF 10:

LONDON PLAGUE GROUND

Country of origin: United Kingdom

IF YOU'RE FEELING A LITTLE BIT
PLAGUE-Y, YOU MIGHT WANT TO STEP AWAY
FROM THAT BUS STOP... UNDER SECTION
33 OF THE PUBLIC HEALTH (CONTROL OF
DISEASE) ACT, 1985, YOU WILL BE ISSUED
A FINE IF YOU TRAVEL WHILE SUFFERING
FROM THE DREADED PLAGUE (EVEN THOUGH
IT WAS ERADICATED ENTIRELY
BY THE 21ST CENTURY).

IF YOU CATCH A SNIFFLE, TRY AN UBER -
THEY'VE SEEN MUCH, MUCH WORSE!

HOW LIKELY ARE YOU TO BREAK THIS LAW?
SCORE YOURSELF OUT OF 10:

‖‖‖ ‖‖‖

HANDS OF THE LAW

Country of origin: Tennessee, USA

KIDS ARE GROWING UP TOO FAST THESE DAYS! AT LEAST, EVERYWHERE EXCEPT TENNESSEE... AND IF YOU'RE A TEACHER IN A TENNESSEE SCHOOL, YOU NEED TO BE VERY CAREFUL WHAT YOU TALK ABOUT TO YOUR STUDENTS, BECAUSE EVEN MENTIONING HAND HOLDING COULD LAND YOU IN SERIOUS TROUBLE. IN FACT, ANYTHING THAT COULD BE DEEMED A 'GATEWAY' TO SEX SHOULD BE AVOIDED AT ALL COSTS — THIS INCLUDES EXPLAINING KISSING, HAND HOLDING AND RELATIONSHIPS AS A WHOLE!

HOW LIKELY ARE YOU TO BREAK THIS LAW?
SCORE YOURSELF OUT OF 10:

LAST STOP 'TIL CHOC

Country of origin: United Kingdom

IF YOU'RE A WOMAN FEELING PECKISH, AND SAT ON A BUS, YOU MAY WANT TO CHOOSE THE TIN OF PRINGLES OVER A MOUTH-WATERING CHOCOLATE BAR.

THIS IS BECAUSE A VERY RANDOM AND OBSCURE LAW FROM THE NINETEENTH CENTURY MADE IT ILLEGAL FOR ANY WOMAN TO EAT CHOCOLATE WHILE TRAVELLING ON PUBLIC TRANSPORT. NOT TO WORRY FELLAS, THE MALE SPECIES IS EXEMPT FROM THIS SUGAR-CRUSHING LAW!

THIS SEXIST LAW IS SO OBSCENE THAT WE'RE SURE NOBODY WILL ACTUALLY NOTICE OR CARE ENOUGH IF YOU LADIES HAVE A LITTLE NIBBLE HERE AND THERE...

HOW LIKELY ARE YOU TO BREAK THIS LAW?
SCORE YOURSELF OUT OF 10:

~~||||~~ ~~||||~~

WE'RE ALL MAD HERE...

Country of origin: United Kingdom

IF YOU'RE THE ONLY LUNATIC LIVING IN YOUR HOME, THEN YOU'RE IN LUCK! AN OLD-TIMEY LAW FROM 1744, THE MADHOUSES ACT, RESTRICTS PROPERTY OWNERS TO ONLY ONE NUTCASE PER RESIDENCE.

BAD NEWS FOR THOSE WANTING TO START A COLLECTION, YOU MUST FIRST APPLY FOR A LICENSE IF YOU WANT TO ADD SOME MORE FRUIT LOOPS TO YOUR ASSORTMENT...

HOW LIKELY ARE YOU TO BREAK THIS LAW?
SCORE YOURSELF OUT OF 10:

~~~~ ~~~~

SLEEPING DRAGONS

Country of origin: Chester, United Kingdom

WE HAVE ONE PIECE OF ADVICE FOR A
WELSHMAN LIVING IN CHESTER... DON'T GO
OUT AFTER DARK.

THIS MIGHT SOUND SILLY AND A LITTLE
PREJUDICED, BUT NONETHELESS, IN 1403
A CURFEW WAS IMPOSED ON THE WELSH,
FORCING THEM NOT TO LEAVE THEIR HOMES
AFTER 7PM. THIS WAS SET IN PLACE
AFTER THE WELSH REVOLTED AGAINST
ENGLAND — AND LOST...

DIDN'T YOU KNOW THAT BEING TUCKED UP
IN BED BY 7PM STOPS ALL
KINDS OF REVOLUTION?

HOW LIKELY ARE YOU TO BREAK THIS LAW?
SCORE YOURSELF OUT OF 10:

~~||||~~ ~~||||~~

POSTMAN S.W.A.T

IF YOU LIKE A GOOD CHAT IN THE
MORNING, YOU'RE ALREADY THE WORST
KIND OF PERSON - I MEAN, AT LEAST LET
PEOPLE DRINK THEIR MORNING COFFEE
FIRST BEFORE INITIATING CONVERSATION.

THOUGH YOU CAN'T GET ARRESTED FOR
BEING A GENERALLY CHATTY PERSON,
YOU COULD BREAK THE LAW IF YOU GET
CHATTING TO YOUR POSTMAN.

JUST LIKE OPENING MAIL NOT ADDRESSED
TO YOURSELF, DELAYING THE POST IS AN
OFFENCE. SO, THE NEXT TIME YOU WANT
TO TALK ABOUT THE WEATHER, TRY
AND CONTAIN YOURSELF...

HOW LIKELY ARE YOU TO BREAK THIS LAW?
SCORE YOURSELF OUT OF 10:

DIRTY DRIVING

Country of origin: Russia

DO YOU LIKE TO GET DOWN AND DIRTY
WHEN IT COMES TO DRIVING? IN BOTH
CHELYABINSK AND MOSCOW, DRIVING A
SUITABLY DIRTY CAR IS ILLEGAL, AND
COULD RESULT IN A FINE OF 2000 RUBLES
(£25) FROM THE POLICE.

THIS IS REPORTED TO BE ENFORCED AS
AN EXCUSE FOR POLICE TO GET 'LUNCH
MONEY', BUT COULD ACTUALLY BE GENUINE
CONCERN FROM THE POLICE – ESPECIALLY
WHEN THE REGISTRATION PLATE IS
COMPLETELY COVERED WITH MUCK!

EVER WATCHED FAST & GLORIOUS? DIDN'T
THINK SO… A BIT OF BIRD C**P ON THE
BONNET NEVER HARMED ANYONE!

HOW LIKELY ARE YOU TO BREAK THIS LAW?
SCORE YOURSELF OUT OF 10:

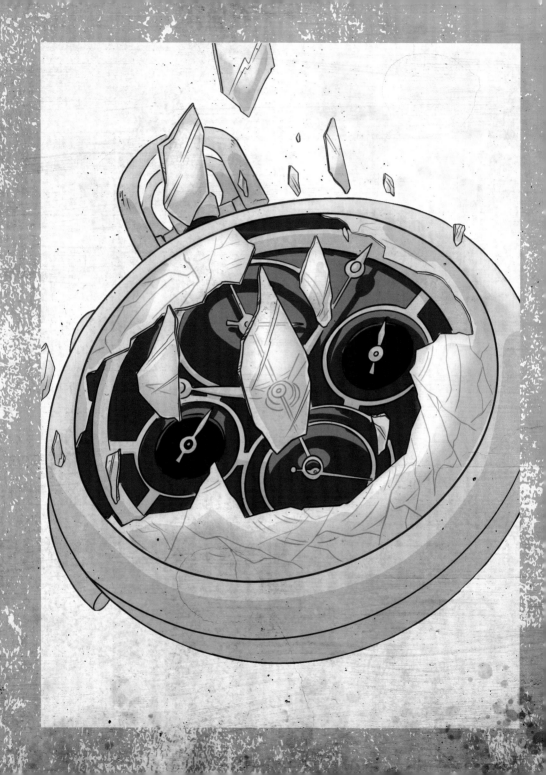

WHAT TIME IS IT?

Country of origin: Madrid, Spain

IN SPAIN'S CAPITAL CITY, MADRID,
IT'S ILLEGAL TO ASK SOMEONE WHAT THE
TIME IS! BETWEEN 3:29PM AND 6:47PM
EVERY DAY, YOU COULD POTENTIALLY BE
PROSECUTED FOR ASKING ANYONE ABOUT
THE TIME, FOR REASONS UNKNOWN. THE
LIKELIHOOD IS THAT THIS IS ANOTHER OLD
LAW THAT IS NO LONGER UPHELD, BUT ONLY
TIME WILL TELL… OR MAYBE IT WON'T -
SHHHH!

SPANISH PRISONS WILL SOON BE PACKED
WITH MURDERERS, THIEVES AND TIME-
TELLING TATTLETALES!

HOW LIKELY ARE YOU TO BREAK THIS LAW?
SCORE YOURSELF OUT OF 10:

SKIRTY BOLOGNESE!

Country of origin: Italy

IF YOU'RE AN ITALIAN MALE WITH A
PASSION FOR FASHION, YOU MIGHT HAVE
AN ABUNDANCE OF FLORAL, PLEATED,
FLOWY SKIRTS IN TOW. OWNING THEM IS
ONE THING, BUT IF YOU DARE TO DRESS
TO IMPRESS IN A SKIRT – NO MATTER HOW
FASHIONABLE, YOU'RE BREAKING THE LAW.

YES, THE FASHION POLICE WILL COME
LOOKING FOR YOU, AND NOT JUST BECAUSE
THAT SKIRT DOESN'T MATCH YOUR SHOES...

HOW LIKELY ARE YOU TO BREAK THIS LAW?
SCORE YOURSELF OUT OF 10:

|||| ||||

FINDERS, KEEPERS

Country of origin: Denmark

IF YOU WANT A CHILD BUT DON'T WANT THE
EFFORT INVOLVED IN MAKING THEM, THEN
DENMARK IS THE PLACE TO GO!

IN DENMARK, A STRANGE (AND QUITE
FRANKLY BIZARRE) LAW IS SET IN PLACE,
STATING THAT IF A PERSON FINDS A LOST
CHILD, THEY ARE ABLE TO HAVE DIBS
ON THE KID IF THEIR CHILD'S PARENT
DOESN'T TURN UP WITHIN 2 HOURS...
NOT GREAT NEWS FOR PARENTS
WITH WANDERING CHILDREN!

**HOW LIKELY ARE YOU TO BREAK THIS LAW?
SCORE YOURSELF OUT OF 10:**

卌 卌

FOR CRYING OUT LOUD!

Country of origin: Paris, France

YOU'VE GONE TO THE SUPERMARKET TO BUY YOURSELF SOME ONIONS FOR TONIGHT'S DINNER AND UPON LEAVING THE SHOP, YOU'RE SURROUNDED BY POLICE… DON'T CRY, THEY'RE NOT GOING TO ARREST YOU (PROVIDED YOU HAVE PAID), THEY'VE COME TO ESCORT YOU AND YOUR ONIONS THROUGH THE STREETS OF PARIS.

THAT'S RIGHT, ANY MAN CARRYING ONIONS IN PARIS MUST BE GIVEN RIGHT OF WAY IN THE STREETS. MAYBE IT'S THE STENCH OF THIS EYE-WATERING VEGETABLE, NOBODY KNOWS WHY…

HOW LIKELY ARE YOU TO BREAK THIS LAW?
SCORE YOURSELF OUT OF 10:

SUN OF A...

Country of origin: Sweden

WE ALL KNOW THAT ONE PERSON WHO JUST *HAS* TO COMPLAIN ABOUT THE WEATHER. "IT'S TOO WARM", "IT'S TOO COLD", "WHERE'S THE SUN GONE?!"... IN ANY OTHER COUNTRY, THEY'RE SAFE, BUT IN SWEDEN, IT'S ACTUALLY ILLEGAL TO COMPLAIN ABOUT 'WISHING IT WERE SUNNY'.

THIS IS BECAUSE IN WINTER, SWEDEN EXPERIENCE VERY LONG HOURS OF DARKNESS, AND WE SUPPOSE HEARING ABOUT THE LACK OF SUN NON-STOP COULD CAUSE SOME PEOPLE TO COMMIT WORSE CRIMES!

HOW LIKELY ARE YOU TO BREAK THIS LAW?
SCORE YOURSELF OUT OF 10:

卌 卌

NAUGHTY NORWEGIANS

Country of origin: Norway

SOMETIMES YOU MAY STUMBLE ACROSS AN
ANCIENT LAW, AND IT'S PRETTY OBVIOUS
WHY IT ISN'T ENFORCED! AND BELIEVE
IT OR NOT, THIS ANCIENT NORWEGIAN LAW
THAT INSTRUCTS MEN TO GO GALLIVANTING
AROUND NEARBY COUNTRIES ON EXPEDITIONS
OF RAPE AND PLUNDER A MINIMUM OF ONCE
EVERY 5 YEARS ACTUALLY ISN'T ENFORCED!
YOU KNOW WHAT THEY SAY, BOYS
WILL BE BOYS!

BRINGING A WHOLE NEW MEANING TO
'LADS ON TOUR'!

HOW LIKELY ARE YOU TO BREAK THIS LAW?
SCORE YOURSELF OUT OF 10:

~~IIII~~ ~~IIII~~

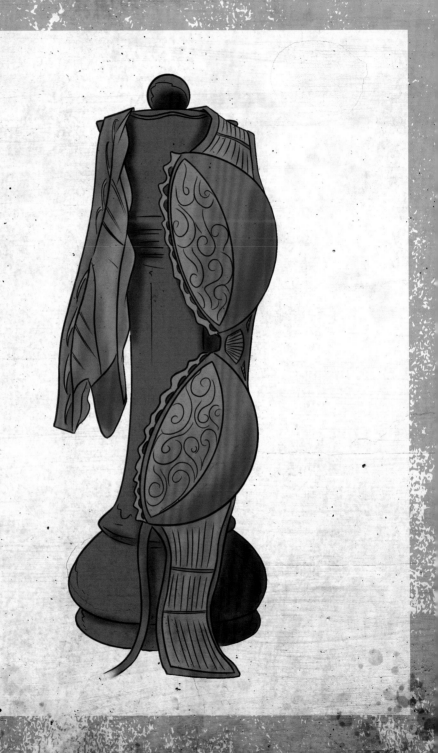

LET'S DO A PAWN-O

Country of origin: Tallinn, Estonia

DO YOU LIKE TO GET A LITTLE FRISKY
DURING FOREPLAY AND WHACK OUT THE
CHESSBOARD TO DECIDE WHO'LL BE ON TOP?
WELL, IN ESTONIA'S CAPITAL, TALLINN,
YOU COULD GET CUFFED (AND NOT IN A
GOOD WAY) IF YOU'RE CAUGHT PLAYING
THIS TACTICAL BOARD GAME...

I MEAN, NOBODY WILL KNOW IF YOU
DO IT IN PRIVATE AND DON'T SCREAM
'CHECKMATE' AT THE WRONG TIME...

A GAME BETWEEN KNIGHTS AND QUEENS,
IT'S PROBABLY BEST TO STEER AWAY
FROM PLAYING CHESS IN THE BEDROOM,
YOU MIGHT END UP LOSING A PIECE...
CHECKMATE!

HOW LIKELY ARE YOU TO BREAK THIS LAW?
SCORE YOURSELF OUT OF 10:

卌 卌

U-F-OH NO!

Country of origin: Châteauneuf du Pape, France

IT IS ILLEGAL TO FLY OVER, OR LAND
FLYING SAUCERS IN CHÂTEAUNEUF-DU-PAPE,
SOUTHERN FRANCE. IT WAS IMPLEMENTED
IN 1954, AND IS RUMOURED TO HAVE
BEEN BROUGHT IN TO GENERATE A BUZZ
ABOUT THE FAMOUS WINE FROM THIS AREA.
BE WARNED - ANY PERSON, HUMAN OR
OTHERWISE, FOUND PILOTING A UFO
WILL BE TAKEN INTO CUSTODY
(AND PROBABLY PROBED)...

IN 2017, THIS BAN WAS EXTENDED,
SO... ALIENS BEWARE!

ARE ALIENS SUBJECT TO THE SAME RULES
AND REGULATIONS AS US? I DON'T KNOW.
BUT ONE SURE FACT IS THAT CHÂTEAUNEUF-
DU-PAPE IS TAKING NO PRISONERS – THAT
IS, THE EXTRATERRESTRIAL KIND!

HOW LIKELY ARE YOU TO BREAK THIS LAW?
SCORE YOURSELF OUT OF 10:

~~HHH~~ ~~HHH~~

SENZA PALLE!

Country of origin: Italy

ANYONE VISITING ITALY SHOULD BE CAREFUL ABOUT WHEN AND WHERE THEY MENTION BALLS. IF YOU'RE ON A GOLF COURSE, YOU'RE PROBABLY FINE TO SHOUT THAT SOMEONE HAS NO BALLS.

SAY IT TO A GRUMPY ITALIAN WITH A MASCULINITY COMPLEX THOUGH, AND YOU'RE IN FOR A HEFTY FINE AND A BLACK EYE - THIS IS BECAUSE ITALIANS ARE SO PRECIOUS ABOUT THEIR GOLDEN GLOBES, THAT TO SAY A MAN HAS NONE WILL BE PUNISHED! THE ONLY TIME IT'S WHOLLY ACCEPTABLE TO TALK ABOUT SOMEONE HAVING NO BALLS, IS WHEN A CHEF SERVES YOU SPAGHETTI WITH NO MEATBALLS!

HOW LIKELY ARE YOU TO BREAK THIS LAW?
SCORE YOURSELF OUT OF 10:

DOZING DONKEY

Country of origin: Arizona, USA

IN ARIZONA, USA, IT'S ILLEGAL TO KEEP A SLEEPING DONKEY IN YOUR BATHTUB… BUT ONLY AFTER 7PM. THIS WEIRD LAW WAS BROUGHT INTO EFFECT AFTER A PUBLIC MENACE CASE IN 1924, WHERE, AFTER FLOODING, THE DONKEY (SLEEPING IN A MERCHANT'S BATHTUB), WAS WASHED AWAY WITH THE FLOOD, AND LOCALS SPENT TIME AND RESOURCES SAVING IT. THE LAW WAS PASSED SHORTLY AFTER!

WHAT A NIGHT-MARE! THAT ASS OF A MERCHANT REALLY MADE A FOAL OUT OF HIMSELF – YOU WON'T FIND US HOUSING A SLEEPING DONKEY IN OUR BATHTUBS AFTER 7PM… NO HAY!

HOW LIKELY ARE YOU TO BREAK THIS LAW?
SCORE YOURSELF OUT OF 10:

~~~~ |||| ~~~~ |||

ONE UGLY MOTHER...

Country of origin: Denmark

COUPLES GET INTO ARGUMENTS ALL THE TIME! THAT BEING SAID, EVEN IF SHE IS A BIT OF A DOG, YOU CAN GET UP TO 1 YEAR IN PRISON BY TELLING YOUR BELOVED WIFE THAT SHE'S "UGLIER THAN HER MOTHER" IN DENMARK. IF YOU THINK THAT'S BAD, IMAGINE WHAT YOUR WIFE AND HER MOTHER WILL DO IF YOU DON'T GET SHIPPED OFF TO PRISON.

MAYBE KEEP YOUR MOUTH SHUT IF YOU DON'T WANT TO BE SENTENCED TO A YEAR OF ROUGH IMPRISONMENT (OR A YEAR OF PAINFUL NAGGING!)

HOW LIKELY ARE YOU TO BREAK THIS LAW?
SCORE YOURSELF OUT OF 10:

FUL-FILL YOUR DUTIES

Country of origin: Denmark

MANY RESTAURANTS AROUND THE WORLD HAVE
FANCY CHALLENGES — EAT YOUR PORTION
WITHIN HALF AN HOUR AND YOU GET
YOUR MONEY BACK...

BUT DID YOU KNOW THAT IN DENMARK, YOU
CAN LEGALLY WALK OUT OF A RESTAURANT
WITHOUT PAYING, AS LONG AS YOU DON'T
FEEL SATISFYINGLY 'FULL' AT THE END OF
YOUR MEAL? YOU'LL LIKELY BE CHALLENGED
THOUGH, SO MAKE SURE YOUR 'OTHER'
STOMACH IS READY FOR YOUR SIXTH COURSE
OF THE MEAL!

THERE'S ONE FLAW IN THIS FUN AND
FILLING LAW... YOU CAN'T ASK FOR A DOGGY
BAG BEFORE YOU LEAVE!

HOW LIKELY ARE YOU TO BREAK THIS LAW?
SCORE YOURSELF OUT OF 10:

‖‖‖ ‖‖‖

HOCUS LOCUST

Country of origin: East Punjab, India

AT THIS POINT, NOTHING SURPRISES US ANYMORE. NOT EVEN GETTING 10 DAYS IN PRISON OR A STEEP FINE FOR FAILING TO WARN OTHERS ABOUT LOCUSTS. YES, YOU READ IT RIGHT. IN EAST PUNJAB, INDIA, ANYONE OVER THE AGE OF 14 IS REQUIRED BY LAW, TO SOUND A 'LOCUST ALARM' BY BEATING ON A DRUM AND MAKING A PROCLAMATION IF THEY SPOT ANY LOCUSTS.

THE EAST PUNJAB AGRICULTURAL PESTS, DISEASES AND NOXIOUS WEEDS ACT OF 1949 IS THE REASON BEHIND THIS ABSURD RULE, SO KEEP YOUR LOCUSTS CLOSE AND YOUR DRUM EVEN CLOSER!

HOW LIKELY ARE YOU TO BREAK THIS LAW?
SCORE YOURSELF OUT OF 10:

~~~~ ~~~~

DROP THE GUM!

Country of origin: Singapore

YOU'LL STOP FEELING LIKE A CHOMP-ION AND MORE LIKE A SOGGY BIT OF GUM IF YOU GET CAUGHT CHEWING EVEN A SINGLE PIECE WHILE IN SINGAPORE.

THE COUNTRY IS SO STRICT, THAT BEING CAUGHT ONCE WILL RESULT IN A $1000 FINE. TWICE, YOU'RE LOOKING AT THAT FINE BEING DOUBLED. AND IF YOU'RE A REPEAT OFFENDER, WELL YOU'LL END UP DOING INTENSE LABOUR, PICKING UP RUBBISH WHILE WEARING A GLAMOROUS SIGN THAT SAYS "I'M A LITTERER".

HOW LIKELY ARE YOU TO BREAK THIS LAW?
SCORE YOURSELF OUT OF 10:

DON'T BE A JERK

Country of origin: Indonesia

IF YOU'RE PARTIAL FOR KNOCKING ONE OUT EVERY NOW AND THEN, YOU MIGHT WANT TO PUT DOWN THE TISSUES AND RECONSIDER YOUR LIFE CHOICES.

WHILE IT'S UNTRUE THAT YOU'LL GET DECAPITATED FOR JERKING OFF IN INDONESIA, YOU WILL GET A SOLID 32 MONTHS IN PRISON TO THINK ABOUT WHAT YOU DID. WHAT YOU DO IN THERE IS NONE OF OUR BUSINESS, BUT IT MIGHT BE A BIT HARDER TO DO BEHIND BARS.

HOW LIKELY ARE YOU TO BREAK THIS LAW?
SCORE YOURSELF OUT OF 10:

HHH HHH

MONKEY BUSINESS

Country of origin: South Bend, Indiana, USA

YOUR PET MONKEY MIGHT BE A 'CHIMP OFF THE OLD BLOCK', BUT IN SOUTH BEND, INDIANA, LETTING A MONKEY SMOKE A CIGARETTE IS A BIG NO-NO. IN 1924, A CHIMPANZEE WAS FINED $5 AFTER BEING FOUND GUILTY OF SMOKING — SO LET THIS BE A WARNING. NO MONKEY BUSINESS - AND NO VAPING EITHER!

STOP MONKEYING AROUND, DO YOU THINK KING KONG GOT TO THE SIZE HE IS BY SMOKING 20 A DAY?!

HOW LIKELY ARE YOU TO BREAK THIS LAW?
SCORE YOURSELF OUT OF 10:

RESPECT YOUR ELDERS

Country of origin: China

DO YOUR PARENTS DRIVE YOU CRAZY EVERY SINGLE HOLIDAY? YOU TRY TO LIMIT PUBLIC INTERACTIONS WITH THEM BECAUSE THEY EMBARRASS YOU, WEARING THEIR SOCKS, SANDALS, AND GARISH T-SHIRTS.

DON'T BE TOO HARSH ON THEM. IT COULD BE WORSE, YOU KNOW... IN CHINA, YOU'RE REQUIRED TO SPEND AN ADEQUATE AMOUNT OF TIME WITH YOUR PARENTS. THE "PROTECTION OF THE RIGHTS AND INTERESTS OF ELDERLY PEOPLE" LAW STATES "THOSE WHO LIVE FAR AWAY FROM PARENTS SHOULD GO HOME OFTEN", SO SQUASH YOUR EGO AND GIVE YOUR PARENTS A BIG SLOPPY KISS!

HOW LIKELY ARE YOU TO BREAK THIS LAW?
SCORE YOURSELF OUT OF 10:

RADIO GA-GA

Country of origin: Canada

CANADA IS KNOWN FOR THEIR PATRIOTIC
WAYS; PUTTING MAPLE LEAVES ON
EVERYTHING, FLAGS ON EVERY CORNER,
ALL DONE WITH A BIG SMILE… BUT NOTHING
TOPS THEIR RADIO RULES.

CANADIAN RADIO STATIONS ARE REQUIRED
BY LAW TO PLAY CANADIAN ARTISTS AT
LEAST 35% OF THE TIME! YES, IF YOU GO
TO CANADA, YOU'LL BE SURE TO HEAR THE
LIKES OF BRYAN ADAMS, JUSTIN BIEBER,
MICHAEL BUBLÉ AND NICKELBACK
(PROBABLY ON REPEAT).

HOW LIKELY ARE YOU TO BREAK THIS LAW?
SCORE YOURSELF OUT OF 10:

|||| ||||

A LOAD OF POOH

Country of origin: Poland

A WRETCHED, UNSCRUPULOUS, GOOD FOR NOTHING CRIMINAL! EXPOSING ONESELF IS A CRIME THAT NEEDS TO BE PUNISHED, AND PUNISHMENT IS WHAT POLAND HAS SERVED!

UNFORTUNATELY, THE CRIMINAL IN ACTION IS ACTUALLY A MUCH LOVED CARTOON BEAR, WINNIE THE POOH, WHO HAS BEEN BANNED FROM SCHOOLS AND PLAYGROUNDS DUE TO THE EXTREMELY RISQUÉ NATURE OF THIS ADORABLE STUFFED BEAR.

IT'S NOT OFTEN PEOPLE GET OFFENDED BY STUFFED TOYS AND CARTOON CHARACTERS, BUT WHEN THEY DO, THEY HIT HARD! BOTTOMS UP WINNIE!

**HOW LIKELY ARE YOU TO BREAK THIS LAW?
SCORE YOURSELF OUT OF 10:**

~~HHH~~ ~~HHH~~

ARMOUR-GEDDON

Country of origin: United Kingdom

YOU BOUGHT YOURSELF A SHINY, NEW, 'REAL' SUIT OF ARMOUR ON AMAZON AND CAN'T WAIT TO GO TO LONDON AND PRETEND TO BE A BRITISH KNIGHT. YOU COULD VISIT THE QUEEN, GET ON THE TUBE AND MAYBE EVEN DO A BIT OF JOUSTING OUTSIDE THE TOWER OF LONDON – NO QUESTIONS ASKED! BUT STEP FOOT IN PARLIAMENT AND YOU'RE SURE TO GET A STERN TELLING OFF (IF THEY REMEMBER THE LAW THAT IS…)

ARMOUR ISN'T VERY FASHIONABLE THESE DAYS, SO THOUGH THIS LAW HASN'T BEEN REVOKED SINCE ITS CREATION IN 1313, YOU PROBABLY WON'T GET A VERY HARSH PUNISHMENT… WE HOPE…

HOW LIKELY ARE YOU TO BREAK THIS LAW?
SCORE YOURSELF OUT OF 10:

G.I NO

Country of origin: Caribbean

THE NEXT TIME YOU GO ON HOLIDAY AND WANT TO PEEK AT SOME HOTTIES ON THE BEACH, MAKE SURE TO KEEP YOUR CAMOUFLAGE SUIT AT HOME. DONNING CAMOUFLAGE IS BANNED IN MANY ISLAND NATIONS, AS IT'S ONLY LEGALLY ALLOWED TO BE WORN BY THE COUNTRY'S MILITARY. IF YOU BRING YOUR BINOCULARS HOWEVER, YOU'RE SURE TO FIND A NICE, STURDY PALM TREE TO SIT UPON!

WHO ARE YOU TRYING TO IMPRESS IN YOUR SAVING PRIVATE RYAN GETUP? GET YOUR SPEEDOS ON AND GIVE THOSE BEACH BABES SOMETHING TO DROOL OVER!

HOW LIKELY ARE YOU TO BREAK THIS LAW?
SCORE YOURSELF OUT OF 10:

|||| ||||

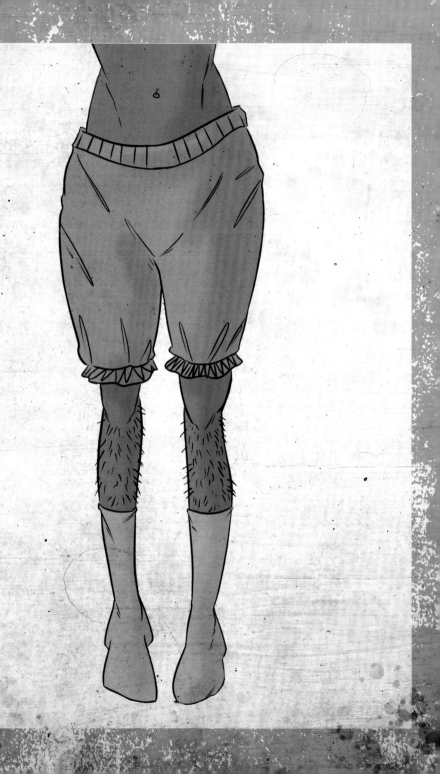

OH PANTS!

Country of origin: Russia

IF YOU'RE PLANNING ON WEARING SOME
SEXY LACE-COVERED UNDERGARMENTS
FOR YOUR THIRD DATE, THEN YOU MIGHT
WANT TO OPT FOR YOUR GRANNY BLOOMERS
INSTEAD. UNFORTUNATELY FOR LADIES (AND
FANCIFUL GENTS), WHAT YOU WEAR UNDER
YOUR CLOTHING COULD GET YOU IN TROUBLE
– FOR 'HEALTH AND SAFETY' REASONS.
WHY? WE HAVE NO CLUE, BUT IN 2014,
A RULE WAS PUT IN PLACE REQUIRING
UNDERGARMENTS BEING MADE WITH A
MINIMUM OF 6% COTTON. OH PANTS!

UNLESS YOU GO AROUND WITH YOUR PANTIES
ON TOP LIKE SUPERMAN, YOU'RE NOT VERY
LIKELY TO GET CAUGHT OUT – UNLESS YOUR
DATE IS A COP.

**HOW LIKELY ARE YOU TO BREAK THIS LAW?
SCORE YOURSELF OUT OF 10:**

GO, GO, GHOST!

Country of origin: China

A GOAT MAYBE? PERHAPS A RABBIT? I FOR ONE WOULD LOVE TO COME BACK AS A CAT AFTER I DIE. IS THIS IN THE REALM OF POSSIBILITY? WHO KNOWS? ONE THING WE DO KNOW FOR CERTAIN, REINCARNATION IS RESTRICTED IN CHINA.

OH YES, IF YOU'RE WANTING TO COME BACK AS A SPIDER OR EVEN A TREE, YOU BETTER HAVE SIGNED PERMISSION FROM THE CHINESE GOVERNMENT, OR THEY'LL... HMM... WHAT WILL THEY DO?

SINCE WE ARE DESTINED TO STAY AROUND AS GHOSTS, WHAT DO YOU SAY WE GO HAUNT THE CHINESE GOVERNMENT FOR THEIR CRAZY LAWS AND RESTRICTIONS? WOOOOOOOO!

HOW LIKELY ARE YOU TO BREAK THIS LAW?
SCORE YOURSELF OUT OF 10:

~~||||~~ ~~||||~~

DON'T WHINE FOR WINE

Country of origin: Bolivia

SINGLE LADIES LISTEN UP! YOU CAN DRINK AS MUCH WINE AS YOU WANT. GO FOR IT! UNFORTUNATELY FOR YOU MARRIED BUNCH, YOU'RE STUCK TO ONE GLASS A DAY.

IT SUCKS, BUT IN BOLIVIA YOU'RE BOUND BY AN OLD, SEXIST LAW BASED ON A STRANGE BELIEF THAT MORE THAN ONE GLASS OF WINE WILL MAKE YOU IMMORAL. HUSBANDS ARE ACTUALLY ABLE TO DIVORCE THEIR WIVES IF CAUGHT DRINKING MORE THAN ONE GLASS... SOUNDS LIKE A WASTE OF WINE TO ME!

THE MORAL OF THE STORY HERE LADIES, IS IF YOU STAY SINGLE, YOU GET MORE WINE AND LESS WHINING!

HOW LIKELY ARE YOU TO BREAK THIS LAW?
SCORE YOURSELF OUT OF 10:

~~||||~~ ~~||||~~

WHAT A WAIST

Country of origin: Japan

IF YOU'RE A FOODIE IN JAPAN, YOU BETTER START COUNTING YOUR CALORIES. TO PREVENT THE RISING OBESITY IN JAPAN'S CIVILIANS, THE JAPANESE GOVERNMENT CREATED THE 'METABO' LAW, WHICH REQUIRES DOCTORS TO ENFORCE AN ANNUAL 'WAIST MEASURING' APPOINTMENT FOR THEIR OLDER PATIENTS.

IF YOU'RE AGED BETWEEN 40 AND 74, YOU NEED TO HAVE WAIST LINES BELOW 33.5 INCHES (FOR MEN) OR 35.4 INCHES (FOR WOMEN) TO AVOID HEFTY FINES - AND A STERN WORD FROM YOUR DOC.

IF YOU'RE ON THE LARGER SIDE OF THE TAPE MEASURE, DON'T WORRY! SUMO WRESTLERS ARE EXEMPT, SO GET TRAINING!

HOW LIKELY ARE YOU TO BREAK THIS LAW?
SCORE YOURSELF OUT OF 10:

~~||||~~ ~~||||~~

UNLUCKY PENNY

Country of origin: Hawaii, USA

ARE YOUR EARS RINGING? BEST CHECK THEM
FOR SOME LOOSE CHANGE! IN THE US STATE
OF HAWAII, IT IS ILLEGAL TO CARRY
LOOSE CHANGE IN YOUR EAR! THIS IS
BECAUSE THIS WAS A SIGN THAT YOU HAD
ILLEGAL SUBSTANCES FOR SALE, SO MAYBE
JUST BRING A PURSE NEXT TIME!

THIS LAW BRINGS A WHOLE NEW MEANING TO
THE PHRASE 'BAD PENNY'!

**HOW LIKELY ARE YOU TO BREAK THIS LAW?
SCORE YOURSELF OUT OF 10:**

~~~~ ~~~~

DIRTY DOG

Country of origin: Capri, Italy

IN THE SUNNY ITALIAN ISLAND OF CAPRI,
THERE IS A LAW THAT ALL DOG OWNERS
MUST PICK UP THEIR PUP'S POOP FROM THE
STREET. WHAT MAKES THIS LAW STRANGE,
HOWEVER, IS THAT IF ANY POOP IS FOUND
UNATTENDED, THE DOG'S OWNER WILL
BE HUNTED DOWN THROUGH A DOGGIE DNA
DATABASE AND FINED! SO DON'T BE DIRTY,
DIG UP THE DOO-DOO!

€2,000 - NOW THAT'S A PRICEY POO!

HOW LIKELY ARE YOU TO BREAK THIS LAW?
SCORE YOURSELF OUT OF 10:

GRIN AND BEAR IT

Country of origin: South Africa

OK SO THIS LAW DOES MAKE SENSE… I
MEAN, WHO IN THEIR RIGHT MIND WOULD
WANT TO WRESTLE A BEAR ANYWAY? YOU'D
BE SURPRISED THOUGH! BEAR WRESTLING
WAS ACTUALLY A VERY POPULAR SPORT, AND
WAS BANNED IN VARIOUS PLACES AROUND
THE WORLD! HOWEVER, BEARS AREN'T EVEN
NATIVE TO SOUTH AFRICA, AND SO THIS
LAW FEELS A BIT OUT OF PLACE!

KEEP THE BEAR HUGS BETWEEN THE BROS!

HOW LIKELY ARE YOU TO BREAK THIS LAW?
SCORE YOURSELF OUT OF 10:

HEIFER-LYSER TEST

Country of origin: Scotland

UNDER THE LICENSING ACT 1872, IT IS
ILLEGAL TO RIDE A COW WHILST UNDER
THE INFLUENCE OF ALCOHOL! IT DOES
MAKE SENSE, BECAUSE THAT SOUNDS LIKE
A DANGEROUS IDEA... ESPECIALLY AFTER
A FEW BEERS! THIS ACT ALSO PROHIBITS
DRUNKS RIDING HORSES AND DRIVING STEAM
TRAINS! MAYBE JUST STICK TO A TAXI.

HAD A CAN? GET OFF YER CATTLE!

HOW LIKELY ARE YOU TO BREAK THIS LAW?
SCORE YOURSELF OUT OF 10:

~~||||~~ ~~||||~~

BIGFOOT

SASQUATCH THIS SPACE

Country of origin: British Columbia, Canada

IT'S NO SURPRISE THAT CANADA'S NATIONAL TREASURE, THE SASQUATCH, IS PROTECTED BY LAW. IN THE 1800S, WHEN SIGHTINGS OF 'BIGFOOT' WERE FIRST REPORTED IN BRITISH COLUMBIA, CANADA, THE PROVINCE ACTUALLY MADE IT ILLEGAL TO KILL IT!

YOU KNOW WHAT THEY SAY ABOUT BIG FEET...

HOW LIKELY ARE YOU TO BREAK THIS LAW?
SCORE YOURSELF OUT OF 10:

~~||||~~ ~~||||~~

BIBLE TASHERS

Country of origin: Alabama, USA

IN THE HEART OF THE BIBLE BELT IN
AMERICA, NOTHING MUST INTERRUPT CHURCH
SERVICE. THIS IS TAKEN SO SERIOUSLY,
THAT IT WAS ACTUALLY BROUGHT INTO LAW
THAT NO FAKE MOUSTACHES CAN BE WORN
IN CHURCHES ACROSS ALABAMA, IN CASE IT
CAUSES A STIR DURING THE SERMON!

I WONDER IF JESUS WAS A HIPSTER...

HOW LIKELY ARE YOU TO BREAK THIS LAW?
SCORE YOURSELF OUT OF 10:

~~||||~~ ~~||||~~

KILT OR BE KILT!

Country of origin: Scotland

THE SCOTTISH ARE FUNNY FOLK, AND
THEIR LAWS MATCH THEIR STRANGE SENSE
OF HUMOUR. THAT BEING SAID, IF YOU'RE
WEARING A KILT IN THE LAND OF TARTAN,
AND DARE TO WEAR YOUR TRUSTY UNDIES
UNDERNEATH, THEN YOU BETTER BRING A
CRATE OF BEER ALONG WITH YOU.

IF YOU GET CAUGHT COVERING YOUR WEE
WILLY WINKY UNDERNEATH THAT VERY MANLY
'SKIRT', THEN YOU'RE GOING TO GET
SHAMED AND FINED TWO CANS OF BITTER.

SO LET YOUR MANHOOD BREATHE! DO YOU
THINK WILLIAM WALLACE GOT AS FAR AS HE
DID WITH HIS PRIVATES CONFINED?

HOW LIKELY ARE YOU TO BREAK THIS LAW?
SCORE YOURSELF OUT OF 10:

𝍷𝍷𝍷𝍷𝍷 𝍷𝍷𝍷𝍷𝍷

CHICKEN RUN

Country of origin: Georgia, USA

IN THE CITY OF QUITMAN, GEORGIA,
CHICKENS WERE RUNNING HAVOC! SO, IN AN
EFFORT TO KEEP THESE CLUCKERS UNDER
CONTROL, A STATUTE WAS BROUGHT IN THAT
WOULD SERVE YOU WITH A FINE IF YOUR
CHICKENS GOT LOOSE! SO, YES – IT IS
ILLEGAL FOR THE CHICKEN TO
ROSS THE ROAD!

HOW LIKELY ARE YOU TO BREAK THIS LAW?
SCORE YOURSELF OUT OF 10:

||||| |||||

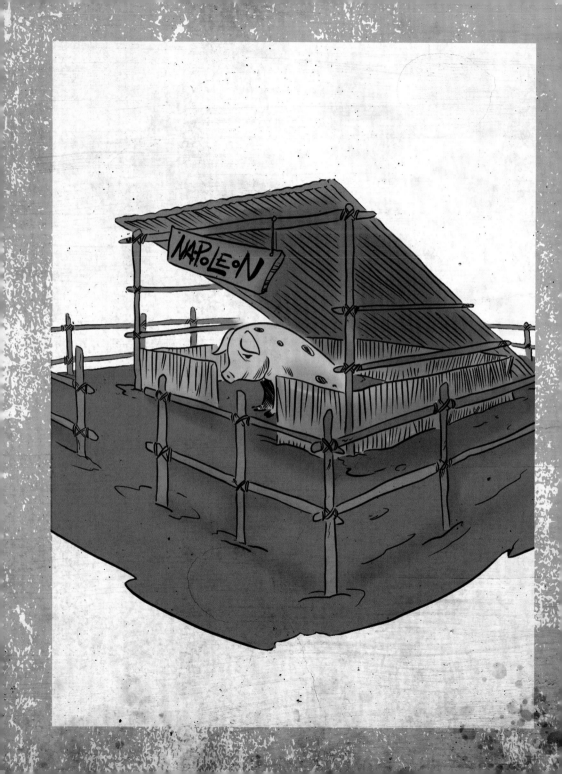

NAPOLEON BONA-PORK

Country of origin: France

THOUGH HE'S BEEN DEAD AND BURIED SINCE 1821, FRENCH LEADER NAPOLEON BONAPARTE STILL LIVES ON WITH A VERY OBSCURE LAW - YOU CAN'T NAME A PIG NAPOLEON! THE FRENCH LOVE THEIR QUIRKY LAWS, BUT THIS ONE IS KIND OF A PIG DEAL FOR THEM, BECAUSE THEY BELIEVE IT WOULD INSULT A HEAD OF STATE, AND WE CAN'T HAVE THAT, CAN WE?

HOWEVER, YOU'LL BE GLAD TO KNOW YOU CAN STILL (LEGALLY) CALL YOUR PET PIG 'AMY SWINE-HOUSE', 'BOAR-IS JOHNSON', OR EVEN 'SWINE-STON CHURCHILL'!

HOW LIKELY ARE YOU TO BREAK THIS LAW? SCORE YOURSELF OUT OF 10:

~~||||~~ ~~||||~~

WHAT A FLOP!

Country of origin: Oklahoma, USA

YOU MIGHT BE WELL KNOWN FOR DRINKING LIKE A GOLDFISH, BUT IN OKLAHOMA, YOU'LL CERTAINLY BE BREAKING THE LAW IF YOU GO DRINKING WITH YOUR FINE FINNED BUDDIES. GETTING A FISH DRUNK SOUNDS ABSURD, BUT IN OKLAHOMA, LAWMAKERS WANT TO MAKE YOUR SATURDAY NIGHTS EVEN MORE BORING.

NOT TO WORRY, THEY NEVER SAID ANYTHING ABOUT GETTING YOUR HAMSTER DRUNK!

GETTING A FISH DRUNK? THEY'LL BE CHATTING BUBBLES AND FLIPPING YOU OFF IN NO TIME!

HOW LIKELY ARE YOU TO BREAK THIS LAW?
SCORE YOURSELF OUT OF 10:

~~~~ |||| ~~~~ |||

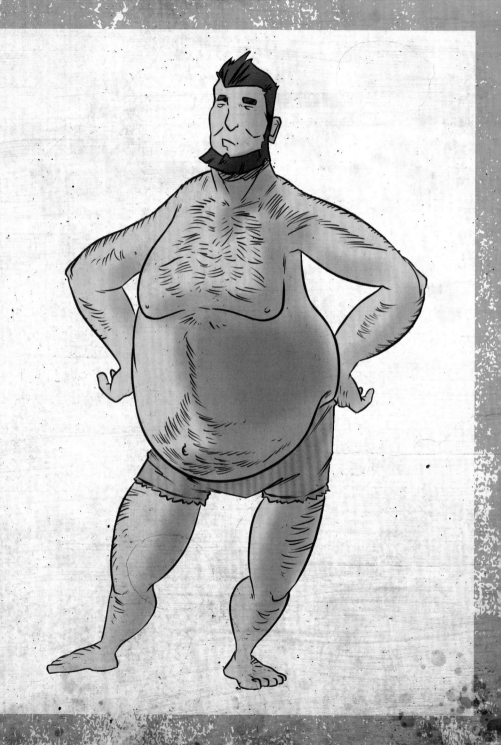

MAKE THE BOYS WINK!

Country of origin: Australia

YOU BOUGHT YOURSELF SOME TRENDY HOT PINK SHORTS. WHAT ARE YOU WAITING FOR?! PUT THEM ON AND STRUT YOUR STUFF! UNLESS YOU'RE IN AUSTRALIA... ON A SUNDAY AFTERNOON... THEN DON'T YOU DARE LEAVE THE HOUSE LOOKING LIKE THAT, YOUNG MAN, OR SO HELP ME!

ONE OF AUSTRALIA'S QUIRKIER LAWS PROHIBITS THE WEARING OF HOT PINK SHORTS IN THREE STATES (NEW SOUTH WALES, VICTORIA, AND QUEENSLAND), BUT ONLY ON SUNDAY AFTERNOONS. THE REASON IS UNKNOWN, THOUGH OUR BET IS SOMEONE JUST REALLY HATES THE COLOUR PINK!

HOW LIKELY ARE YOU TO BREAK THIS LAW?
SCORE YOURSELF OUT OF 10:

𝍩𝍪 𝍩𝍪

VICE-CREAM

Country of origin: Alabama, USA

GOT A SWEET TOOTH AND NOTHING LEFT TO LOSE? FILL YOUR BACK POCKETS WITH ICE-CREAM! IN ALABAMA, IT'S ILLEGAL (RIGHTLY SO) TO WALK DOWN THE STREET WITH AN ICE-CREAM CONE IN YOUR BACK POCKET. THIS IS DUE TO HORSE THIEVES USING THIS METHOD TO LURE AWAY HORSES WITHOUT BEING CAUGHT STEALING.

IF YOU LIKE THE STICKINESS OF MELTED ICE-CREAM ALL OVER YOUR PANTS, BUT DON'T WANT TO PAY A FINE, THEN THE FRONT POCKETS ARE PERFECTLY LEGAL, YOU SICKO!

HOW LIKELY ARE YOU TO BREAK THIS LAW?
SCORE YOURSELF OUT OF 10:

~~~~ ~~~~

FEEL THE HEAT

Country of origin: Peru

IF CHILLIES TICKLE YOUR PICKLE, AND YOU JUST SO HAPPEN TO BE AN INMATE IN A PERUVIAN PRISON (UNLIKELY, BUT NOT IMPOSSIBLE...), THEN THIS LAW IS JUST FOR YOU! IN 1973, PERU'S INTERIOR MINISTER HAD A BRILLIANT IDEA. HE BELIEVED THAT SPICY FOODS – WAIT FOR IT... WOULD AROUSE PRISON INMATES SEXUAL DESIRES CONSTANTLY! YES, WHO KNEW SRIRACHA COULD MAKE YOU HORNY?

OUR ADVICE, WASH YOUR HANDS WELL BEFORE YOU REGRET ADDING A BIT OF SPICE TO THE MOOD!

HOW LIKELY ARE YOU TO BREAK THIS LAW?
SCORE YOURSELF OUT OF 10:

𝍷𝍷𝍷𝍷𝍷 𝍷𝍷𝍷𝍷𝍷

OH B*LLOONS!

Country of origin: Canada

CANADA IS A STRICT COUNTRY, BUT NOTHING REALLY BEATS THIS TONGUE-TWISTER OF A TORONTO LAW...
ARE YOU READY?

IT'S ILLEGAL TO CURSE WHILE BEING NAKED AND RELEASING BALLOONS IN A PUBLIC PARK. YES. CURSING, NUDITY, BALLOONS AND PARKS WERE ALL MENTIONED IN THE SAME SENTENCE. WE'RE NOT TOO SURE HOW THIS LAW CAME ABOUT OR WHO MIGHT WANT TO BREAK IT, PERHAPS A NUDIST CLOWN WHO HAS TOURETTE'S AND REALLY LOVES PARKS?
WE'LL LET YOU DECIDE.

HOW LIKELY ARE YOU TO BREAK THIS LAW?
SCORE YOURSELF OUT OF 10:

~~||||~~ ~~||||~~

DUMP IN THE DAYTIME

Country of origin: Switzerland

IF YOU'RE THE KIND OF PERSON WHO LIKES
TO INCORPORATE HAVING A NUMBER 2 INTO
THEIR EVENING ROUTINE, THEN I HAVE
BAD NEWS FOR YOU! FLUSHING THE TOILET
AFTER 10PM IS SURPRISINGLY ILLEGAL!

THIS IS DUE TO NOISE POLLUTION RULES
THAT REQUIRE TENANTS TO REDUCE THE
NOISE THEY MAKE BETWEEN THE HOURS
OF 10PM AND 6AM! WHILST THIS LAW IS
RARELY ENFORCED, IF YOUR LANDLORD
WANTED THERE COULD BE REPERCUSSIONS
FOR A LATE-NIGHT FLUSH!

HOW LIKELY ARE YOU TO BREAK THIS LAW?
SCORE YOURSELF OUT OF 10:

~~||||~~ ~~||||~~

PUCKER UP!

Country of origin: Nevada, USA

BEEN NOTICING HOW THE MOUSTACHE HAS MADE ITS WAY BACK INTO FASHION OVER RECENT YEARS? YOU WON'T BE WRONG – THAT 70S UPPER LIP SLUG HAS BEEN MAKING PEOPLE SWOON AS OF LATE! HOWEVER, FOR RESIDENTS OF EUREKA, NEVADA, THE MOUSTACHE DEFINITELY ISN'T IN!

ACTUALLY, THEY HAVE SUCH A VENDETTA AGAINST THE SUPPOSEDLY BACTERIA-HARBOURING HAIRY FEATURE THAT IT IS ILLEGAL TO KISS A WOMAN IN PUBLIC IF YOU HAVE A MOUSTACHE!

HOW LIKELY ARE YOU TO BREAK THIS LAW?
SCORE YOURSELF OUT OF 10:

HHH HHH

TERMINATE YER TOOTIN'

Country of origin: Malawi

MALAWI, IN THE SOUTHEAST OF AFRICA, BROUGHT IN THE AIR FOULING LEGISLATION IN 2011, MAKING IT ILLEGAL FOR ANYONE IN MALAWI TO 'FOUL THE AIR'... MEANING THAT, UNDER A TECHNICALITY... FARTING COULD BE SEEN AS ILLEGAL! TRY TO SAVE IT FOR THE LOO...

BEANS, BEANS, GOOD FOR THE HEART, THE MORE YOU EAT, THE MORE YOU GET IN SERIOUS TROUBLE WITH THE LAW...

HOW LIKELY ARE YOU TO BREAK THIS LAW?
SCORE YOURSELF OUT OF 10:

LOVE THY NEIGHBOUR

OK, WE'VE ALL HAD NEIGHBOURS THAT HAVE REALLY GOTTEN UNDER OUR SKIN. MAYBE THEY LIKE TO MOW THE LAWNS AT 6AM? OR PERHAPS THEIR FENCE IS JUST A LITTLE FAR INTO YOUR BOUNDARY? WHATEVER IT IS, TRY TO REFRAIN FROM DUSTING OFF THE CANNON TO GET YOUR OWN BACK! AS PART OF S.55 OF THE

METROPOLITAN POLICE ACT 1839, IT IS ILLEGAL TO FIRE A CANNON WITHIN 300 YARDS OF A DWELLING, SO SAVE YOUR CANON FIRING FOR THE BATTLEFIELD!

HOW LIKELY ARE YOU TO BREAK THIS LAW?
SCORE YOURSELF OUT OF 10:

||||| |||||

TO SKI, OR NOT TO SKI!

Country of origin: Switzerland

SKIING IS NOT FOR THE FAINT-
HEARTED, AND THAT GOES FOR POETS TOO.
SWITZERLAND IS SO AGAINST RECITING
POETRY WHILE SKIING DOWN A MOUNTAIN,
THAT THEY ACTUALLY MADE IT ILLEGAL... A
SHAME REALLY, BECAUSE THE SWISS ALPS
ARE A SIGHT MANY POETS WOULD LOVE TO
CHANT ABOUT... SO NEXT TIME YOU WANT TO
SKI DOWN THE EIGER, REMEMBER TO LEAVE
EDGAR ALLAN POE AT HOME!

AFTER SKIING ON THE MOUNTAIN FLOOR,
I HEARD A RAPPING AT MY CABIN DOOR.
"A VISITOR," I MUTTERED,
"TAPPING AT MY DOOR — WITH ONLY A FINE
AND NOTHING MORE."

HOW LIKELY ARE YOU TO BREAK THIS LAW?
SCORE YOURSELF OUT OF 10:

卌 卌

WHY THE LONG FACE?

Country of origin: Milan, Italy

STEMMING FROM THE AUSTRO-HUNGARIAN ERA, IT'S A LEGAL REQUIREMENT FOR ALL CITIZENS OF MILAN, HAPPY OR SAD, TO SMILE AT ALL TIMES. DON'T WORRY - THERE ARE CERTAIN EXCEPTIONS, INCLUDING FUNERAL GOERS AND HOSPITAL WORKERS. WHILST THIS JAW-CRAMPING LAW ISN'T TECHNICALLY IN PLACE ANYMORE, IT HAS NEVER OFFICIALLY BEEN REPEALED, SO IF YOU'RE HEADING TO MILAN, DON'T LEAVE YOUR GRIN AT HOME!

IT MAKES US WONDER IF YOU'RE REQUIRED TO SAY 'CHEESE' FOR YOUR MUGSHOT... EITHER WAY, WE SUPPOSE YOU'D HAVE TO GRIN AND BEAR IT!

HOW LIKELY ARE YOU TO BREAK THIS LAW?
SCORE YOURSELF OUT OF 10:

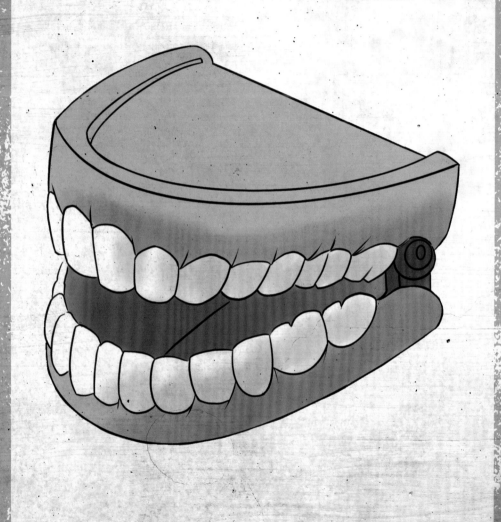

GUMMY MUMMY

Country of origin: Vermont, USA

IN VERMONT, WOMEN MUST GET THEIR
HUSBAND'S WRITTEN APPROVAL BEFORE
GETTING FALSE TEETH! THIS IS ANOTHER
LAW THAT DATES BACK TO BEFORE WOMEN
WERE LEGALLY ENTITLED TO MAKE BOLD
DENTAL DECISIONS ON THEIR OWN TERMS.
BELIEVE IT OR NOT, THIS LAW IS
ACTUALLY STILL IN THE BOOKS!

ALL I WANT FOR CHRISTMAS IS MY
TWO FRONT TEETH!

HOW LIKELY ARE YOU TO BREAK THIS LAW?
SCORE YOURSELF OUT OF 10:

~~IIII~~ ~~IIII~~

THE WAY YOU'RE GOING
WILL YOU END UP IN

PRISON?